Awesome Inventions
You Use Every Day

Fun Food Inventions

NADIA HIGGINS

LERNER PUBLICATIONS COMPANY
MINNEAPOLIS

Lerner Publications Company
A division of Lerner Publishing Group, Inc.
241 First Avenue North
Minneapolis, MN 55401 U.S.A.

Website address: www.lernerbooks.com

Library of Congress Cataloging-in-Publication Data

Higgins, Nadia.
Fun food inventions / by Nadia Higgins.
p. cm. — (Awesome inventions you use every day)
Includes index.
ISBN 978–1–4677–1091–6 (lib. bdg. : alk. paper)
ISBN 978–1–4677–1682–6 (eBook)
1. Food—History—Juvenile literature. 2. Inventions—History—Juvenile literature. I. Title.
TX355.H488 2014
641.309—dc23   2012040813

Manufactured in the United States of America
1 – PP – 7/15/13

CONTENTS

INTRODUCTION:

THAT MYSTERY INGREDIENT

Quick—what's your favorite food? *Why?*

Sure, it's yummy. You'd snarf it out of a dog bowl if you had to. But there's something else—a mystery ingredient. Food scientists refer to it as Fun with a capital *F*.

What creates a high fun factor in food? Often it's a texture thing. Think crispy, gooey, juicy, and fizzy to name a few.

How you eat food also matters. How fun is licking frozen stuff on a stick? And don't forget the awesomeness that is dipping and dunking.

How do inventors come up with fun foods? Sometimes it's by accident. They messed up. Luckily, they kept their eyes open to life's delicious mistakes. Other times, they were looking to make a fortune so they just kept on working at it until they hit the jackpot. Still other times they put the cherry on top of somebody else's good idea.

You know what's almost as fun as eating fun foods? Reading about them. So let's dig in!

KETCHUP

It's 1727. You're in England, and you want some ketchup. Or rather, *katchop*, as they spelled it back then. Your mutton slab needs some zing.

Luckily, the first ketchup recipe in English has just come out. You crack open your new copy of E. Smith's *The Compleat Housewife*. You turn the crinkly pages. You find the recipe despite the weird spelling. Then—"EEEEEeeeeeeew!" you scream. "Anchovies . . . cloves . . . mushroom juice? Art thou kidding me?"

Even worse, you'll have to wait at least one hundred years for ketchup to get good. But what can you expect? This condiment comes from a word that means "the brine of pickled fish." Long ago, people in China were flavoring their foods with a sauce they called *ke-tsiap*. The fishy stuff spread throughout Southeast Asia. British explorers brought it back to England in the late 1600s. Then English cooks said, "This sauce isn't gross enough. What can we do?" They added mushrooms and walnuts, mostly. They used lots of salt, vinegar, and wine to make sure the muddy stuff didn't "spoil."

Meanwhile, over in the United States, ketchup got even funkier. One person started adding tomatoes. These red veggies didn't seem like a half-bad ingredient for ketchup after that. In 1812 the first known tomato ketchup recipe hit the presses. Sure, it called for brandy instead of vinegar. But little by little, ketchup got tangier, sweeter, smoother, and redder. These days, you're practically a freak of nature if you don't eat ketchup!

French fries and Ketchup—some things just go together.

Presenting five useless facts about Ketchup:

1. Ketchup can make pennies amazingly shiny.
2. Heinz sells 11 billion Ketchup packets a year.
3. Banana Ketchup is huge in the Philippines.
4. Ketchup is about one-fourth sugar.
5. Heinz Ketchup flows from a glass bottle at a speed of 0.028 miles (0.045 Kilometers) per hour. The speed is actually tested in a lab. If the Ketchup is too fast, it's thrown out.

POTATO CHIPS

So many wonderful things can inspire a great invention. Genius, passion, or a worthy cause. So just what inspired potato chips—one of America's favorite snacks? Grumpiness.

In 1853 chef George Crum was having a bad day. It was summer tourist season in lovely Saratoga Springs, New York. Crum was in charge of the kitchen at the fancy Moon's Lake House. And some customer had sent his fries back. He said they were too soggy. He wanted them cut thinner.

"Fine!" we can imagine Crum saying. "Hmmmph." He sliced up a thinner batch and sent it out.

A few minutes later, though, the fussy customer sent back *that* batch.

"FINE!" (This time Crum probably yelled.) He sliced those potatoes paper thin. He fried them until they were golden brown. In those days, fries were eaten with a knife and a fork. Well, that was out of the question with these crispy buggers. Then, in a final parting shot, Crum salted the heck out of them. Ha!

Guess what? The customer *loved* Crum's potatoes. In fact, he put in another order. Soon Saratoga Chips were a local delicacy. In 1860 Crum opened his own restaurant. Each table got a basket of his famous chips.

But Crum never made a fortune on his invention. The big payoff went instead to businessperson Herman Lay. In the 1930s, Lay started a company that made the very first national brand of potato chips. It was then that the snack really took off. These days, the average American eats about 6 pounds (3 kilograms) of chips every year.

Chef Crum invented potato chips when he overcooked some fries to get back at a fussy customer.

Who can resist the satisfying crunch of potato chips?

BUBBLE GUM

Chomping for kicks must be some kind of primal human thing. Ancient peoples from all over the globe liked to keep their jaws moving. They chewed on everything from animal skins to dried tree saps.

Modern gum hit U.S. drugstores in the 1870s. Back then, black licorice flavor was all you got. No wonder people kept tweaking the recipe. Gum got softer. It lasted longer. Mint and fruit flavors entered the mix. But something was still

missing. What was it? Oh, yes—bubbles. What was gum without the option of blowing it up as big as your head?

Enter the world's first bubble gum . . . Blibber-Blubber! Frank Henry Fleer introduced his invention in 1906. Too bad the gum was as lame as its name. It was hard to chew and too sticky.

But the quest was on. As it turned out, the Fleer Chewing Gum Company had a secret weapon—their accountant, Walt. In his spare time, Walter E. Diemer experimented with gum recipes. In 1928 Walt struck gold—pink gold.

"It was an accident," he later said. "I was doing something else and ended up with something like bubbles." That could happen to anybody, really. In Walt's case, the result was the perfect balance of stretchy and sticky. He used pink dye because that's all he had on hand. He named it Dubble Bubble. 'Nuff said.

ON APRIL 24, 2004, CHAD FELL SET THE GUINNESS WORLD RECORD FOR BLOWING ONE OF THE BIGGEST BUBBLES EVER. It was a whopping 20 inches (51 centimeters) in diameter!

Chad's secret? He said he used the roof of his mouth to form a nice, thick wad of gum. Then he put his tongue through the gum just once and started puffing.

Black Jack

ADAMS
Black Jack
CHEWING GUM
AMERICAN CHICLE COMPANY

"Good old licorice flavor!"

THE HOLD-UP

At first, gum came only in licorice flavor.

DOUGHNUTS

The idea seems kind of obvious. Take some dough and fry it. Even in ancient times, people knew that carbs + fat = yumminess.

Dutch settlers brought fried dough to North America in the early 1700s. People started adding egg yolk to the recipe. That made for a delicious doughnut. But there was a problem. The outside cooked faster than the inside. The middle was a greasy puddle.

"Why didn't they just poke a hole in the middle?" you ask. Easy for you to say. Obviously, they were waiting for the doughnut hole to be invented.

That's right. Someone actually invented that area of non-dough. He's even got a plaque.

Here's what we know. Hanson Gregory, a Maine ship captain, made a doughnut hole in 1847. But beyond that, the story's a total mystery! Stories about Gregory have more holes than a dozen Krispy Kremes. In one, he's steering a ship while munching on a fried cake. Then—shiver his timbers!—the mighty sea rises up. He needs both hands on the wheel. How will he save his crew and his doughnut? Thinking fast, he skewers his treat on one of the wheel's spokes. Talk about solving two problems at once!

When Gregory was an old man, he gave a tamer story to the *Boston Globe*. In this one, his stomach ached after eating

a whole bunch of really greasy doughnuts. There had to be a better way, he thought. So, he took the tin lid off a box to use as a cookie cutter. Then he "cut into the middle of that doughnut the first hole ever seen by mortal eyes."

In the name of all things crispy, America thanks you, Mr. Gregory!

Hanson Gregory invented the doughnut hole in 1847. Here he poses with a glazed doughnut, complete with a large hole.

What would a doughnut be without a hole?

FORTUNE COOKIES

What would you do if you went out for Chinese and *didn't* get a fortune cookie? You'd feel ripped off. But if you were in China, that would be totally cool. In fact, most Chinese people don't even know about fortune cookies. These funky cookies are an all-American treat—with Japanese beginnings.

In the 1800s, a religious community in Japan made rice cookies with paper fortunes inside. Those cookies were larger and darker than the ones we know in modern times. They were flavored with salty miso and sesame seeds.

In 1914 a Japanese American man started serving fortune cookies at his café in San Francisco, California. The snacks were a hit. They spread among the Japanese American community. Shortly thereafter, they caught on with Chinese Americans too.

Chinese food has long been popular in the United States. Fortune cookies proved to be the perfect finish to a plate of chicken almond ding. These days, they are a staple at more than forty thousand Chinese restaurants across the country.

You will start a new adventure.

JUST HOW DO THEY GET THE FORTUNE INSIDE?

Well, fortune cookies are mostly sugar, flour, and water. In modern times, most of the cookies are made by machines. The batter is poured into little cups. Then a metal plate keeps the dough flat as it cooks for just a few minutes. At this point, the cookie is a warm, floppy circle. Vacuums place the paper fortune onto the cookie. Metal fingers fold the dough. As it cools, it hardens. It's ready for you to crack open.

ICE-CREAM SUNDAE

Yes, ice-cream sundaes did start out as ice-cream *Sundays*, in case you've ever wondered. So why did their name change? Here's the story.

In the 1880s, ice-cream sodas were a hit. They featured ice cream, soda water, and syrup. But slurping up a fizzy beverage was considered rude on Sunday. That was, after all, the day when many Americans went to worship services at church. In the Midwest, some towns even passed what were known as blue laws. These laws banned all kinds of "misbehavior" on Sundays. This included dancing, drinking alcohol, gambling—and sipping soda.

Obviously, people needed to find a new ice-cream treat to enjoy after church. "What if we just lose the soda?" several people thought. (Who exactly thought it first is a matter of hot debate.) And presto—the ice-cream *Sunday* was born.

But then people started thinking it was wrong to name a dessert after the holiest day of the week. So someone changed the name to ice-cream *sundae*. The treat has gone by this name ever since.

Soon ice-cream lovers were enjoying the dessert every day of the week. Meanwhile, ice-cream parlors started going all out. They added whipped cream, nuts, and—in 1892—the cherry on top.

SUNDAY
(Church)

Strict laws used to limit what kinds of things people could do on Sunday.

You can enjoy this ice-cream treat on any day of the week!

PEZ

It's a dark time in candy history. The year is 1927. The place is Vienna, Austria. Eduard Haas III has just invented PEZ. But it comes in just one flavor—peppermint. And to get one, you open a *plain tin box*.

That's right. No clown head spitting the candy into your palm. No Yoda, no Tweety Bird . . . not even Santa.

PEZ comes from the German word for peppermint, *pfefferminz*. Back then, the humble candy brick was meant for adults who wanted to quit smoking. (The treat was supposed to take their minds off their smoking habit.)

Fast-forward to 1948. Oscar Uxa not only has the most fun name ever. He also comes up with the PEZ dispenser. OK, so it looks a little like a lighter. But the magic has begun.

Still, the PEZ people have a problem. Their product is not selling well in the United States. What can they do? "I know!" says one really smart person. "Let's sell PEZ to kids!"

Soon the company is cranking out fruity flavors that go inside fun toy dispensers. A freaky blue robot is among the first. Over the next six decades, more than five hundred kinds of PEZ dispensers will arrive on the scene. Think everything from George Washington to SpongeBob to a baseball glove. By 2013, 99 percent of U.S. kids are officially bummed if they don't have PEZ.

PEZ dispensers come in an amazing variety!

PEZ once was sold in tin boxes such as these.

PEZ: TRUE OR FALSE?

1. PEZ sells 1.8 billion candies each year.
2. The best-selling PEZ toy of all time is Santa.
3. Past PEZ flavors have included coffee, chocolate, and bacon.
4. A PEZhead is a person who eats tons of PEZ.

Answers: 1) False (It's 4.2 billion!); 2) True; 3) False (Just the bacon part.); 4) False (It's someone who collects PEZ dispensers.)

PEPPERMINT

SPEZIAL

MICROWAVE POPCORN

Raytheon Company was looking for something to do with their magnetron tubes. Yes, that is how the story of microwave popcorn begins. See, a magnetron tube was a thing that gave off radiation. And so does a microwave.

Magnetron tubes were a key part of radar, which had been developed during World War II (1939–1945). U.S. soldiers used it to track down enemy planes at night.

So how did magnetron tubes go from wartime tool to inspiration for a favorite snack? Well, by 1945, it was clear that the war was about to end. That meant magnetron sales were about to tank. Raytheon had to find another way to make money.

One day, scientist Percy Spencer was experimenting with magnetrons in his lab. The next thing he knew, the answer was melting in his pocket. He noticed something brown and gooey there. It was his candy bar! What could have made it melt? Spencer figured it had to be a magnetron.

Good scientist that he was, Spencer wanted to make sure his theory was correct. He sent out for popcorn kernels. He put them in a bag and held it by a magnetron. Yesssss! The kernels popped into perfect white fluffiness. Spencer decided to invent an oven that would cook in the same way a magnetron did. This oven, of course, would be the microwave.

The first microwaves were as big as refrigerators. After more than twenty years, microwaves finally got down to a practical size. These days, people everywhere use the ovens to pop up the perfect batch of popcorn. Spencer holds patents for both microwave ovens and the microwavable popcorn people cook in them.

Microwave popcorn is a tasty and popular snack.

The Waldorf Astoria Hotel used this giant microwave to cook food for its guests in the late 1940s.

MICROWAVE DINNERS

Many inventions led to the creation of microwave dinners. There was the microwave, obviously. Percy Spencer took care of that in 1945. But a whole bunch of other stuff you'd never think needed to happen . . . well, it *did* need to happen. Check it out.

1. Flash freezing food. Clarence Birdseye invented that in 1923. He got the idea from Inuit fishers in the Arctic. Their catch froze instantly as it was pulled out of the water. When it thawed, it was flaky—not mushy. That's key for your microwave dinner.

2. Heatable trays. Thank William L. Maxon and his Strato-Plates for these. Maxon invented Strato-Plates—or plates on which you could both heat and eat your food—for troops during World War II.

3. Compartments. Gerry Thomas was gung-ho about separating the foods on a plate. He came up with a divided tray for Swanson & Sons in the early 1950s. He wasn't the first to separate his peas from his mashed potatoes, but he was the most successful.

4. Foods that all take the same amount of time to cook. Think about it. You press 5, and all your different foods come out cooked to perfection. This was a big hurdle. Betty Cronin at Swanson worked out the kinks in the early 1950s.

Starting in 1954, Swanson's "TV dinners" wowed America. Here was a meal you could buy in one convenient package. But the tray was metal, which leads us to . . .

5. The right kind of plastic for the microwave. Swanson switched from foil trays to plastic in 1986. Beeeeep. The microwave dinner was official!

Gerry Thomas shows off the special tray he invented for Swanson in the early 1950s.

Clarence Birdseye, inventor of flash freezing, experiments with food at the Birdseye company in 1943.

GRAHAM CRACKERS

Eat lots of veggies. Get plenty of fresh air. Wash regularly.
Health guru Sylvester Graham gave some great advice in the
1820s and the 1830s. But he didn't stop there. No, he had
to get all weird about it. Like saying his health rules were the
only way to heaven. Or saying ketchup would make you crazy.
Or even saying—and this one was key—that white flour was not
just bad for you but *evil*.

This last belief spurred Graham to invent a flour made from
coarsely ground wheat. He called it Graham flour, which was
used to make Graham bread. It was all the rage among his
followers—called Grahamites.

But Graham's views also earned him plenty of enemies
(Grahamemies?). Angry bakers showed up at his talks in Boston
and New York. Some brought tar and feathers. They taunted
him. They called him "a nut among the crackers." Oh, snap!

In fact, Graham was the boss of crackers. In 1829 he
invented the Graham cracker. The healthful snack had tons
of fiber. It caught on . . . and got less and less healthful.
The graham crackers we know and love today are full of
white flour. Next time you munch on one of these delicious
rectangles, listen carefully. Do you hear something? That's
Sylvester Graham turning over in his grave.

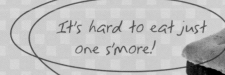

It's hard to eat just one s'more!

S'MORE IS SHORT FOR "SOME MORE"— as in, "I gotta have some more of this gooey-crunchy sweet perfection!" This graham cracker dessert became a camping favorite in the early 1900s. By then, Nabisco was selling graham crackers in a box. Marshmallows had become a grocery item too.

We don't know who came up with s'mores. But it figures that the Thin Mint people would play a hand. The first printed recipe for s'mores appeared in the 1927 Girl Scout Handbook.

The graham crackers of today aren't as healthful as earlier versions of the snack.

Nabisco
Grahams
-ORIGINAL-
made with 8g of whole grain*
per serving

NET WT 14.4 OZ (408g)

POPSICLES

In 1905 eleven-year-old Frank Epperson was relaxing on his porch in San Francisco, California. He was mixing himself a soda—which is something people did back then. He was stirring his cup of water and drink mix with a stick. Then he went inside without drinking it. He forgot to come back and clean up before bed, and he couldn't even blame TV.

That night was really cold. The next morning, Frank found that the soda had frozen. He yanked on the stick and—voila!

The soon-to-be famous Epsicle ice pop was born!

OK, not quite. Frank had some fun making Epsicles for his friends and neighbors. But he didn't get serious for another seventeen years or so. By then he had kids. They were always asking for "Pop's 'sicle," so the story goes. Epperson realized that had a better ring to it.

In 1924 Epperson got a patent for his invention. By then he knew exactly what it took to make a perfect ice pop. The crystals had to be nice and even. The treat had to be just hard enough, not too drippy. It had to not fall off the stick.

A year or so later, Frank Epperson sold the rights and the name to his invention. Then he basically spent the rest of his life smacking his forehead and yelling, "Why? Why? Why?" Popsicle pops went on to become one of the most successful treats ever. These days, more than two billion of them are sold each year.

Popsicle inventor Frank Epperson enjoys one of the frozen goodies with his granddaughter, Nancy Epperson, in 1973.

ROOT BEER

Root beer was invented out of necessity. It's true. Here are three stories to prove it.

Story 1: Back in the Middle Ages (500–1500), a monk in Belgium noticed something really important. People who drank beer were healthier than people who drank water. Of course, in those days, "fresh" water was a cesspool of germs. Beer had been boiled, which killed most germs. That's how it got its reputation as a "health" drink. Except it made you woozy. Drinks known as small beers became a thing for kids. These drinks weren't fermented long enough to become boozy, just fizzy. They were brewed with handfuls of roots and spices—just like root beer.

Story 2: The Pilgrims kept their beverages in wooden kegs. Water stored this way went bad, but beer didn't. At first, the Pilgrims didn't have the barley needed to make strong beer. So they made small beers with berries, roots, and spices. Beer was considered the most healthful drink for children—much better than milk!

Story 3: Pharmacist Charles Hires was trying to find a medicine that could cure all kinds of health woes. Instead, he found deliciousness, which may be the same thing.

During his honeymoon in New Jersey, Hires was served a wonderful tea with sassafras bark and herbs. Back home, Hires got to work. How could he make it even more delicious? He worked with the recipe until he had a syrup with more than twenty-five ingredients. In 1876 he showcased his product at a fair in Philadelphia, Pennsylvania. He told people to mix it with soda water, which was considered super healthful in those days. It was a hit! By 1893 he was selling Hires Root Beer in bottles and making a fortune.

An ice-cold mug of root beer hits the spot on a hot day.

A young boy lugs Hires Root Beer home in 1955.

GLOSSARY

blue law: a law that limits what people and businesses in the United States can do on Sundays. In the 1880s, blue laws in the Midwest banned the sale of soda water.

condiment: a spread or a sauce that you add to food to give it flavor. Ketchup is the third most popular condiment in the United States, after mayonnaise and salsa.

fermented: chemically broken down in a way that results in alcohol as well as gases (bubbles). Beer is fermented.

fiber: material in food that is hard to digest and therefore helps push the food through the intestines. As Sylvester Graham knew, fiber is good for you.

Inuit: a group of closely related peoples who are native to parts of Alaska, Canada, and Greenland. Clarence Birdseye got the idea of flash freezing from observing Inuit culture.

miso: a salty brown paste made from fermented soybeans. Miso is a popular ingredient in Japanese cooking.

patent: a document given by the government that says an inventor is the only one allowed to use or sell his or her invention for a certain number of years. Patents protect inventors from imitators.

radar: a system of using radio waves to figure out where objects are. The development of radar by Raytheon Company led to the invention of the microwave.

radiation: invisible waves of energy. Microwaves are a form of radiation.

sassafras: a medium-sized tree that grows in the eastern part of North America. Sassafras bark was a traditional ingredient of root beer. These days, most root beers use artificial sassafras flavoring.

FURTHER INFORMATION

Discovery Kids—Food Myths
http://kids.discovery.com/tell-me/mythbusters/food-myths
Can people really slip on banana peels? Can you swim as fast in syrup as in water? Find out the answers to freaky food questions.

Donovan, Sandy. *Does It Really Take Seven Years to Digest Swallowed Gum? And Other Questions You've Always Wanted to Ask*. Minneapolis: Lerner Publications Company, 2010. Find out the truth behind seventeen of the most common "facts" passed around at recess.

Guinness World Records
    http://www.guinnessworldrecords.com
    Some people really know how to play with their food! Check out
    "Farthest Milk Squirting Distance," "Largest Pizza Base Spun in 2
    Minutes," and other amazing human achievements.

KidsHealth—Your Digestive System
    http://kidshealth.org/kid/htbw/digestive_system.html
    Find articles like "Love Your Liver" and "Are Your Bowels Moving?" on
    this fun site about what happens to food after it goes down the hatch.

Murphy, Jim. *Weird & Wacky Inventions*. New York: Sky Pony Press,
    2011. Read the true story behind the "used-gum receptacle" and
    other crazy inventions that never quite made it.

National Geographic Kids—Recipes
    http://kids.nationalgeographic.com/kids/activities/recipes
    Learn how to make fortune cookies using an egg carton as well
    as Cherries in the Snow, Lucky Smoothie, and other fun foods.

Rosenberg, Pam. *How Did That Get to My Table? Ice Cream*. Ann
    Arbor, MI: Cherry Lake, 2010. Ice cream starts with milk at a
    dairy farm, but it goes through a lot of steps before it ends up in
    your sundae. Read all about it in this colorful book.

Travel Channel's *Bizarre Foods with Andrew Zimmern*
    http://www.travelchannel.com/tv-shows/bizarre-foods
    Pigeon pie, lamb's tongue, armadillo barbecue . . . these are
    just a few dishes that have been featured on *Bizarre Foods*.
    Check out videos, photos, recipes, and more on this wild site.

SOURCE NOTES

6.   Johnny Acton, Tania Adams, and Matt Packer, *Origin of
       Everyday Things*, (New York: Sterling, 2006), 130.

10.   Ibid., 39-40.

12.   John T. Edge. *Donuts: An American Passion*, (New
       York: Penguin, 2006), http://books.google.com/
       books?id=qP1TmIfv3_oC&q=greasy+sinkers#v=snippet&q=g
       reasy%20sinkers&f=false (January 15, 2013).

24.   Jean Farmer, "The Rev. Sylvester (Graham Cracker)
       Graham: America's Early Fiber Crusader," *Saturday Evening
       Post*, March 1, 1985, 32.

INDEX

PHOTO ACKNOWLEDGMENTS

The images in this book are used with the permission of: © Deborah Jaffe/Digital Vision/Getty Images, p. 5; © iStockphoto.com/Floortje, p. 7 (top left); © Westend61/Getty Images, p. 7 (top right); © iStockphoto.com/wdstock, pp. 7 (bottom left), 11 (top), 15 (bottom), 19 (middle), 25 (middle); © Alptraum/Dreamstime.com, p. 7 (bottom right); Courtesy of the Saratoga Springs History Museum, p. 9 (top); © Msphotographic/Dreamstime.com, p. 9 (bottom); © Image Source/Getty Images, p. 11 (middle); © Transcendental Graphics/Archive Photos/Getty Images, p. 11 (bottom); Courtesy Camden Public Library, Edward J. Walsh History Center Collection, p. 13 (top); © Ivonnewierink/Dreamstime.com, p. 13 (bottom); © Justin Sullivan/Getty Images, p. 15 (top); © iStockphoto.com/sumnersgraphicsinc, p. 15 (middle); © Transcendental Graphics/Archive Photos/Getty Images, p. 17 (top); © iStockphoto.com/DNY59, p. 17 (bottom); © age fotostock/SuperStock, p. 19 (top); Courtesy of PEZ Candy Inc., p. 19 (bottom); © Gvictoria/Dreamstime.com, p. 21 (top); © Bettmann/CORBIS, pp. 21 (bottom), 23 (bottom), 27 (top); AP Photo/Mike Fiala, p. 23 (top); © iStockphoto.com/Ashok Rodrigues, p. 25 (top); © Food and Drink/SuperStock, p. 25 (bottom left); © iStockphoto.com/Roel Smart, p. 25 (bottom right); © iStockphoto.com/Jill Fromer, p. 27 (bottom); © iStockphoto.com/Eddie Berman, p. 29 (top); © Lambert/Archive Photos/Getty Images, p. 29 (bottom).

Front cover: © iStockphoto.com/Jill Fromer.

Main body text set in Highlander ITC Std Book 13/16.
Typeface provided by International Typeface Corp.